Gluten Free Slow Cooker Cookbook

50 Healthy Everyday Meals + 10 Bonus Desserts

Gluten Free Slow Cooker Cookbook

By

F.L.Clover

Copyright ©2014

Cover photograph by Darius Dzinnik

This ebook is licensed for your personal enjoyment only. This ebook may not be re-sold or given away to other people. If you would like to share this book with another person, please purchase an additional copy for each recipient. If you're reading this book and did not purchase it, or it was not purchased for your enjoyment only, then please return to your favorite retailer and purchase your own copy. Thank you for respecting the hard work of this author.

Copyright Notes

No part of this publication may be reproduced in any form or by any means, including printing, photocopying, or otherwise without prior written permission of the copyright holder.

Table of Contents

About Us	1
Introduction	2
Chapter One: Breakfast Recipes	4
1. Peach Oatmeal	4
2. Congee (Asian Rice Porridge)	6
3. Cherry Oatmeal	7
4. Quinoa Casserole	8
5. Pumpkin Cinnamon Oatmeal	9
6. Blueberry Clafoutis	10
7. Pear Butter	12
8. Chocolate Risotto	13
9. Maple Walnut Oatmeal	14
10. Spinach and Ham Casserole	15
Chapter Two: Lunch Recipes	16
1. Beef and Cabbage	16
2. Cheesy Chicken	17
3. Lentil Soup	18
4. Salsa Pork Tenderloin	19
5. Chicken Dumpling Soup	21
6. Jambalaya	22
7. Sweet Potatoes	23
8. Pork Chille	24
9. Split Pea Soup	25
10. Turkey Meatloaf	26
11. Stuffed Peppers	27
12. Slow Cooker Roast	28

13. Bean Soup	29
14. Exotic Chicken Dish	30
15. Chili Verde	31
16. Mac & Cheese	32
17. Hungarian Soup	33
18. Smoky Soup	34
19. French Onion Soup	36
20. Salmon Pasta Casserole	37
Chapter Three: Dinner Recipes	38
1. Turkey Chili	38
2. Orange Chicken	39
3. Pumpkin Parsnip Soup	40
4. Beef Carnitas	41
5. Potato Ham Chowder	42
6. Creamy Kale Chicken	43
7. Mexican Cauliflower Soup	44
8. Mashed Cauliflower	45
9. Citrus Turkey	46
10. Buttery Chicken	47
11. Pumpkin Chili	48
12. Jack Chicken	49
13. Spicy Shrimp with Rice	50
14. Four Bean Stew	51
15. Split Pea Sausage Stew	52
16. Beef Stroganoff	53
17. Turkey Cranberry Stew	54
18. Shrimp Arrabiata	55
19. Pork Chops	56

20. Onion and Corn	57
Chapter Four: Desserts & Beverages	58
1. Baked Apples	58
2. Date Pudding	59
3. Brownie Squares	60
4. Strawberry Rhubarb Crisps	61
5. Applesauce	62
6. Coconut Cherry Bars	63
7. PB Chocolate Cake	64
8. Dulce de Leche	66
9. Apricot Cherry Compote	67
10. Apple Mulled Cider	68
Conclusions	69
Photo credits	70
Other books from F.L. Clover	75

Gluten-Free Slow Cooker Cookbook

F.L.Clover

About Us

We are a publishing company specializing in the publication of recipe books.

We publish new authors, as well as renowned ones, and take pride in the quality of our products. Our goal is to provide readers with recipes that are easy to prepare, taste great and contain no gluten, as well as with meals that are inspired from the Paleo lifestyle. If you're willing to experience the benefits of a gluten-free / Paleo lifestyle and diet, make sure to check our best sellers and outstanding new titles.

Our books cover an array of recipes in the Asian, European and American cuisine, from traditional ones to exotic dishes, and from slow cooker to raw gluten-free or Paleo recipes. We know how challenging a life without these grains or dairy can be, so we put all our energy and enthusiasm in creating recipes for breakfast, lunch and dinner, as well as flavorful desserts and beverages.

We prefer affordable dishes that can be prepared with ingredients available world-wide, as we want to please all our readers, regardless of their location. The personal touch that we add to our recipes results in an enjoyable cooking experience and flavorful, mouthwatering and appealing dishes.

Introduction

Restrictive diets don't work in the long run, we all know this, and except for a few lost pounds, they don't do much in terms of improving your overall health or appearance. This is why I'm not into dieting and I prefer sticking with a healthy lifestyle that allows me not only to easily maintain my weight, but also to enjoy delicious foods without worrying about my weight and health.

How is this possible? The simple and short answer is: by switching to a gluten-free lifestyle. Before going gluten-free, my health was average. I was constantly feeling tired and energy deprived, dealing with digestive issues, from bloating to cramps and discomfort after eating bread, cereals, biscuits and pretty much anything that contained gluten. Not to mention I was having a really hard time controlling my sugar cravings (I have a terrible sweet tooth, I must admit).

Despite avoiding junk foods, eating limited amounts of sweets and working out regularly, my weight wasn't ideal either. And above all these, I was moody most of the time, unable to focus right after meals and stressed by the idea that I probably have to starve myself if I want to see some improvements.

So one day I decided it was time for a change, but I wanted a less dramatic approach – I wasn't ready to give up desserts and really didn't want to end up counting calories and eating only green veggies. I did a lot of research before going gluten-free, and I must say it's the best decision I ever made. I recovered my health, vitality and well-being!

It's true: health comes from the inside, and if you eat bad foods, regardless of what their labels say, you'll feel bad. Health is more than counting calories and avoiding junk products: if you're intolerant to gluten and eat bread, but have an otherwise balanced diet, you'll still feel and look bad, because your body wasn't designed to digest this compound.

F.L.Clover

This book is not about weight loss, but I want you to realize that cooking gluten-free recipes means more than leaving an ingredient out of your dishes: it's a conscious and responsible decision, and a big step towards a healthier lifestyle.

I created this book to help you avoid some of my mistakes. After removing gluten from diet, I found myself in an unpredicted but common situation: my food options seemed really limited and I started asking myself how and if I'll be able to survive without pasta, bread, breakfast cereals and so on. But as I kept reading and researching this niche, I discovered new ingredients I could use to make my dishes taste heavenly, and I also gathered a list of food replacements.

My collection of gluten-free recipes extended quickly, so I want to share some of my favorite slow cooker GF recipes with you. Switching to a gluten-free lifestyle can be overwhelming if you're not used with cooking and aren't familiar with the numerous products you can use as replacements. This is why I'm sharing these recipes – they're tested, delicious and healthy, and they'll teach you how to choose your ingredients after removing gluten from your diet. Moreover, all of them are created for the slow cooker, so if you enjoy flavorful, saucy, creamy, mouthwatering dishes, this book is surely for you.

Feel free to experiment with other ingredients and to adjust the taste based on your personal preferences, but try to stick with the recommended cooking times and ingredient amounts. Preparing a food using the slow cooker requires more patience, but the reward is definitely worth the time and effort.

Happy cooking, and if you enjoy this book, make sure to connect with me via social media and to check the other publications from F.L. Clover.

Chapter One: Breakfast Recipes

1. Peach Oatmeal

Ingredients
- 2 cups oats
- 1 cup coconut milk
- 3 cups water
- 1 cup peaches
- 1/4 cup honey
- 1/4 cup coconut oil or butter
- 1 tablespoon apple cider vinegar
- 1 teaspoon cinnamon and cardamom, each
- 1/2 teaspoon salt
- 1 teaspoon vanilla extract

Method
1. The day before preparing the dish, coat the bottom of the slow cooker with butter or coconut oil and add the oats, apple cider vinegar and water. Let the oat soak for 12 hours, without draining, then add the remaining ingredients in the crock pot.
2. Turn on the slow cooker and set it on low. Let it cook for 7 to 8 hours, then transfer to plates and serve with honey and coconut milk.

F.L.Clover

*Check the label to make sure the oats are gluten free, as some products might be cross contaminated.

2. Congee (Asian Rice Porridge)

Ingredients
- 1 cup white rice
- 6 cups homemade chicken broth
- 3 cloves garlic, sliced

Method
1. Before starting the preparation, rinse the rice several times until the water runs clean.
2. Place the rice, broth and garlic in the slow cooker and turn it on. Cook for 8 hours, on low temperature.
3. Serve as it is or topped with coriander, scallions or fish sauce.

3. Cherry Oatmeal

Ingredients
- 2 cups gluten-free oats
- 1 cup almond or coconut milk
- 3 cups water
- 1/4 cup coconut oil or melted butter
- 1 cup cherries
- 1 teaspoon vanilla extract
- 1/2 teaspoon salt
- 1 teaspoon honey, optional

Method
1. The day before preparing the dish, grease the bottom of the slow cooker with butter or coconut oil and add the oats and water. Let it soak for 12 hours and don't drain.
2. Add the cherries, vanilla, coconut milk and salt and turn the slow cooker on, on low temperature. Cook for 8 hours.
3. Serve as it is or topped with honey. For a thinner consistency, add more coconut milk.

*Make sure the oats are gluten free, as some products might be cross-contaminated.

4. Quinoa Casserole

Ingredients
- 2 cups quinoa
- 1 cup broccoli
- 1 cup sweet peppers
- 3 garlic cloves, chopped
- 2 cups tomato paste, homemade
- 4 cups water or more if needed, to cover all the ingredients
- 1 cup goat cheese, optionally

Method
1. Add the quinoa, broccoli, peppers and garlic in the slow cooker and cover with tomato paste. Add 4 cups of water, or more if needed, until all ingredients are fully covered.
2. Turn the slow cooker on low temperature and leave it on for 8 hours.
3. Transfer to plates and serve as it is or with goat cheese on top.

5. Pumpkin Cinnamon Oatmeal

Ingredients
- 1 cup oats
- 4 cups water
- 1 cup pumpkin puree (homemade or unsweetened)
- 1 tablespoon butter or coconut oil for a vegan recipe
- 1 teaspoon vanilla extract
- 1 teaspoon cinnamon
- 1/2 teaspoon nutmeg
- 1 tablespoon honey or maple syrup
- 1 cup plain yogurt, optionally

Method
1. The day before preparing the dish, grease the slow cooker with coconut oil or butter and add the oats and water. Let it soak for 12 hours and don't drain.
2. Put all the remaining ingredients (except for yogurt, if using) in the slow cooker and turn it on at low temperature.
3. Cook for 8 hours (or for 4 hours on high). Serve as it is or topped with yogurt and extra nutmeg.

*You can replace the honey with applesauce, but make sure it's homemade and doesn't contain too much sugar.

6. Blueberry Clafoutis

Ingredients
- 1.5 cups blueberries
- 1 cup milk
- 1/2 cup almond flour
- 1/2 cup gluten-free pancake mix or rice flour
- 2 eggs
- 2 tablespoons butter or coconut oil
- 1/2 cup sugar
- 1 teaspoon vanilla extract
- Pinch salt
- Lemon zest, optionally

Method
1. Grease the bottom and inside of the slow cooker with coconut oil or butter and sprinkle with almond flour. Add the blueberries and set aside.
2. In a small bowl, add the eggs, sugar, salt and pancake mix and whisk to obtain a smooth consistency. Add the milk and vanilla extract and whisk again until the mixture is smooth.
3. Pour the mixture into the slow cooker to cover the berries and add lemon zest on top, if using.
4. Turn the slow cooker on and cook on low for 4 hours. After 4 hours, check to see if the clafoutis has browned around the edges. The dish should look puffy and the center should be set when it's ready. If needed, cook for 1 hour more on low temperature.

F.L.Clover

    5. Transfer to plates and sprinkle with sugar if wanted.

7. Pear Butter

Ingredients
- 5 pounds pears, peeled
- 4 cardamom pods
- 1/4 cup water
- 1 teaspoon ginger

Method
1. Core and chop the pears, then add them with the remaining ingredients in the slow cooker.
2. Turn the crock pot on and leave it to low temperature for 8 to 10 hours.
3. Transfer the mixture into a blender and puree to obtain a smooth consistency.
4. Transfer the puree back in the slow cooker and cook for 2 to 4 hours more, or until the butter becomes thicker and reaches the desired consistency.
5. Serve with gluten-free bread or crackers.

8. Chocolate Risotto

Ingredients
- 1 cup white rice
- 3 cup coconut milk
- 2 cups water
- 1/2 cup coconut oil
- 1 tablespoon cacao, unsweetened
- 1 teaspoon vanilla extract
- 1/4 teaspoon salt
- 1 cup chocolate chips, semi-sweet
- 1/4 cup brown sugar, optionally
- Strawberries or raspberries, optionally
- Whipped cream, optionally

Method
1. Grease the bottom of the slow cooker with coconut oil, then add the rice, 2 cups milk and water. Turn the slow cooker on and let it cook for 2 hours on high temperature.
2. Once most of the liquid is absorbed, and the rice is tender, add the remaining milk, cacao, vanilla, salt and sugar if using. Stir to incorporate well and cook again for 2 hours on medium.
3. Check to see if there's enough liquid inside the slow cooker - if it's been absorbed, add some extra water or coconut milk and mix the chocolate chips. Let the dish sit for about 15 minutes, uncovered, and stir to combine evenly.
4. Transfer to serving plates and serve as it is or with whipped cream and berries on top.

9. Maple Walnut Oatmeal

Ingredients
- 2 cups coconut or almond milk
- 1 cup oatmeal
- 2 cups water
- 1/2 cup chopped pears
- 1/2 cup chopped walnuts
- 2 tablespoons applesauce or maple syrup
- 1/2 cup coconut oil or butter
- 1/2 teaspoon salt
- Cocoa ice-cream, optionally

Method
1. Grease the bottom of the slow cooker with coconut oil or butter and add the oat and water until well covered. Let it soak for 8 hours and don't drain.
2. Add the milk, pears, salt and applesauce and turn the slow cooker on, cooking for 5 to 6 hours on low.
3. Stir in the walnuts and incorporate well, then let it cool for 15-20 minutes.
4. Transfer to plates and serve as it is or with extra walnuts and cocoa ice-cream on top.

10. Spinach and Ham Casserole

Ingredients
- 6 eggs
- 1 cup diced ham
- 1/2 cup plain yogurt
- 1/4 cup milk
- 1 cup baby spinach
- 1 cup shredded jack cheese
- 1/2 cup diced mushrooms
- 1 teaspoon garlic powder
- 1/2 teaspoon salt
- Cooking spray or butter

Method
1. Spray the slow cooker with cooking spray or grease it with butter and set aside.
2. Meanwhile, whisk the eggs, yogurt, salt, milk and garlic powder in a bowl until well incorporated. Stir in the cheese, mushrooms, ham and spinach and transfer all ingredients to the slow cooker.
3. Turn the crock pot on and let it cook for 3 to 4 hours on medium. Check to see if the eggs are set and cook for 1 hour more, on low, if needed. Transfer to plates and serve as it is or with fresh tomatoes.

Chapter Two: Lunch Recipes

1. Beef and Cabbage

Ingredients
- 1 pound potatoes, halved
- 1 small green cabbage, cut into 8 wedges
- 3 pound corned beef brisket
- 2 medium carrots, cut into smaller chunks
- 3 cups water
- 1 bay leaf
- 2 cloves garlic
- 1 teaspoon brown sugar
- 1 teaspoon salt

Method
1. Add the potatoes, garlic, carrots and bay leaf into the slow cooker. Put the beef, salt and sugar on top and cover with water.
2. Turn the slow cooker on and cook on low, for 8 to 10 hours. Add the cabbage and cook for another hour, on low temperature.
3. Remove from the slow cooker and let cool for 10 to 15 minutes, then transfer onto plates and discard the bay leaf. Serve as it is.

2. Cheesy Chicken

Ingredients
- 6 pieces boneless chicken breast
- 1 cup cheddar cheese
- 1 can mushroom
- 1 cup chicken broth
- 1/2 cup parmesan cheese
- 1 can diced green chilles
- 1 cup milk
- 1 teaspoon garlic powder
- 1 teaspoon salt, optionally

Method
1. Place the chicken pieces into the slow cooker, add garlic and salt if using and pour the chicken broth, mushrooms, cheddar cheese, milk and chilles on top. Mix to incorporate well and turn the slow cooker on, cooking for 3 to 4 hours on high or for 6 to 8 hours on low.
2. Check to see if the meal is well done and add a layer of parmesan on top. Cook for another hour on low temperature. Transfer to plates and serve as it is.

3. Lentil Soup

Ingredients
- 1 cup lentils, sorted and rinsed
- 1 can diced tomatoes
- 5 cups water
- 2 cups packed spinach
- 1 cup plain yogurt
- 1 tablespoon olive oil
- 1 onion, chopped
- 1/2 cup unsalted peanuts
- 3 cloves garlic, minced
- 1 teaspoon cumin seeds
- 1 teaspoon coriander, paprika and salt each

Method
1. Add the oil, cumin seeds, lentils, tomatoes, spinach, garlic, onion and yogurt into the slow cooker and cover with water.
2. Turn the slow cooker on and cook for 3 to 4 hours on low temperature.
3. Stir in the remaining ingredients and mix to incorporate well. Cook for one more hour on low temperature. Transfer to plates and serve as it is or with extra yogurt on top.

4. Salsa Pork Tenderloin

Ingredients
- 2 pounds pork tenderloin
- 1 cup chicken stock
- 6 cloves garlic, minced
- 2 peppers, cut into smaller pieces
- 1 cup sour cream, low fat
- 1 pound fresh tomatillos, halved
- 1 large onion
- 2 tablespoons olive oil
- 1/2 cup cilantro
- 1 teaspoon salt, black pepper, ground cumin and dried oregano each

Method
1. Turn the broiler on and place the halved tomatillos on a baking sheet. Broil for 5 to 10 minutes, on each side. Remove from the oven and place them into a food processor. Puree and set aside.
2. In a bowl, mix the seasonings and rub the pork tenderloin with this mixture. When it's well coated, sear the meat on all sides for about 5 to 10 minutes, then place the meat in the slow cooker.
3. Add the chicken stock, onions, garlic and tomatillo puree and stir to incorporate well. Season with salt and pepper to taste and turn the slow cooker on, cooking for 6 to 8 hours on low temperature.

Gluten Free Slow Cooker Cookbook

4. Transfer to a plate and slice the meat, then pour the sauce on top and serve with sour cream on top.

5. Chicken Dumpling Soup

Ingredients
- 1 pound skinless chicken breast, cut into small pieces
- 2 cups chicken broth, homemade if possible
- 10 ounces mixed veggies
- 1 cup gluten-free flour such as rice flour
- 1/2 cup milk
- 1 onion
- Salt and pepper to taste

Method
1. Put the chicken, veggies and onion into the slow cooker and add the chicken broth on top. Stir to combine well and turn the slow cooker on, cooking for 5 to 6 hours on low temperature.
2. In a small bowl, mix the flour and milk to obtain a thicker consistency and add tablespoonfuls of this mixture into the soup. Cook for 1 more hour on low temperature.
3. Season with salt and pepper to taste and serve as it is or with coriander.

6. Jambalaya

Ingredients
- 1 pound chicken sausage
- 1 pound chicken breast, cut into smaller cubes
- 1 pound peeled shrimp, cooked
- 1 can diced tomatoes
- 1 package pepper stir-fry mix
- 1 package jambalaya rice mix
- 2 stalks celery, chopped
- 2 cups water

Method
1. Cut the meat and halve the sausages lengthwise, then place them all into the slow cooker together with the peppers, tomatoes, celery, rice mix and water. Mix to incorporate well and turn the slow cooker on, cooking on low temperature for 6 hours.
2. Stir in the remaining ingredients and cook for 1 hour more on low temperature. Serve as it is.

7. Sweet Potatoes

Ingredients
- 4 sweet potatoes, large
- 1 tablespoon butter
- 1 tablespoon canola oil
- 1 teaspoon cinnamon and ground nutmeg, each
- 1 tablespoon honey
- 3 tablespoons water

Method
1. Scrub the potatoes and pierce with a fork on all sides.
2. In a bowl, mix the oil, butter and seasonings to incorporate well, then add the honey and mix to obtain a thicker paste.
3. Coat the potatoes with this mixture and place in the slow cooker, cooking on low temperature for 4 to 6 hours.
4. Check for tenderness and transfer to plates, serving the dish as it is or with sour cream on top.

8. Pork Chille

Ingredients
- 2 pounds pork meat, cut into smaller cubes
- 1 cup chicken broth, homemade if possible
- 2 cups potatoes, cut into smaller cubes
- 8 corn tortillas (make sure they're gluten-free)
- 1 bottle salsa, gluten-free
- 1 onion, sliced
- 1 green pepper, chopped
- 2 limes, cut into smaller pieces
- 1 tablespoon canola oil
- Salt and pepper to taste

Method
1. In a bowl, season the pork with salt and pepper.
2. In a large skillet, heat the oil and add the pork in batches, searing on all sides until caramelized. Center should still be raw, so don't overcook it.
3. Transfer the meat into the slow cooker and add the broth, onion, pepper and salsa. Turn the slow cooker on and cook for 8 hours on low temperature.
4. Add the potatoes and remaining ingredients except for tortillas and cook for one hour more, on low temperature. Transfer to plates and serve with tortillas and stewed veggies if desired.

9. Split Pea Soup

Ingredients
- 1 pound split green peas
- 4 cups veggie stock
- 1 cup baby carrots, chopped
- 3 celery stalks, chopped
- 2 cloves garlic, minced
- 1 onion, chopped
- 2 bay leaves
- 1/2 cup fresh parsley, chopped
- 1 tablespoon dried thyme
- 2 cups water
- 1 tablespoon olive oil
- Salt and pepper to taste

Method
1. Put the peas in a bowl and cover with water. Let them soak for 2 to 4 hours, then drain, rinse and transfer them to the slow cooker.
2. Add the celery, onion, garlic, carrots, thyme, parsley and bay leaves. Season with salt and pepper to taste and add the veggie stock.
3. Turn the slow cooker on and cook for 8 to 9 hours on low temperature, until the peas are well cooked. Serve as it is.

10. Turkey Meatloaf

Ingredients
- 1 pound lean ground turkey
- 2 cups brown rice, cooked
- 1 egg
- 1/2 cup sliced mushrooms
- 1/2 cup oats
- 1/2 cup chicken broth, homemade
- 2 cups tomato sauce, homemade or unsweetened
- 1 tablespoon seasoning to taste
- 1 tablespoon mustard

Method
1. In a bowl, combine the meat with the egg, onions, mushrooms, mustard and seasoning and mix to form into a round loaf.
2. Add the sauce and broth into the slow cooker and place the meatloaf on top, spooning the sauce over it.
3. Turn the slow cooker on and cook on low temperature for 6 to 8 hours. Spoon sauce over the meat after 2 hours.
4. Check for doneness and cook for 1 more hour if needed, on low temperature. Serve with brown rice.

*Make sure that the oats are gluten-free, some products might be cross-contaminated.

11. Stuffed Peppers

Ingredients
- 1/2 cup rice
- 4 large bell peppers
- 8 ounces ground beef
- 1 large onion, finely chopped
- 1 jar marinara sauce
- 1/4 cup raisins
- 1 teaspoon ground cumin
- 1 tablespoon red wine vinegar
- 1/4 teaspoon cinnamon
- Chopped parsley to garnish

Method
1. In a bowl, combine the sauce with cinnamon, cumin and vinegar. Pour half of the mixture into the slow cooker.
2. In another bowl, mix the beef, onion, raisins, rice and remaining sauce. Spoon the mixture into the peppers and place them into the slow cooker.
3. Turn the slow cooker on to low temperature and cook for 6 to 8 hours. Check if the peppers are tender and filling is cooked.
4. Serve with sauce on top and garnish with parsley.

12. Slow Cooker Roast

Ingredients
- 2 pounds beef chuck roast
- 1 pound small potatoes
- 4 ribs celery, chopped
- 8 ounces baby carrots
- 1 can beef broth, reduced-sodium
- 1/2 cup rice flour
- 1 cup chopped onion
- 3 tablespoons tomato paste
- 1 teaspoon salt, dried thyme and black pepper, each

Method
1. Coat the slow cooker with cooking spray and add the rice flour. Pour the beef broth and whisk to obtain a smooth mixture. Add the tomato paste and seasonings.
2. Add the meat, carrots, onion, potatoes and celery in the slow cooker and spoon sauce over the beef, to cover well.
3. Cook on low temperature for 7 to 8 hours, until the meat is tender. Serve as it is or with veggies alongside.

13. Bean Soup

Ingredients
- 1.5 cups beans
- 1 can diced tomatoes
- 2 garlic cloves, minced
- 4 carrots, chopped
- 1 onion, chopped
- 2 cups chicken broth
- 7 cups water, divided
- 1/2 cup grated Romano cheese
- 1 tablespoon dried rosemary
- 1/2 teaspoon salt
- 1/2 cup olive oil, optionally

Method
1. The day before preparing the dish, add the beans into a bowl and cover with 4 cups of water. Soak overnight, drain and rinse.
2. Place the beans into the slow cooker and add the tomatoes, onions, rosemary, carrots and tomatoes. Add the remaining water and cook on low temperature for 4 to 6 hours.
3. Check if the beans are tender, season with salt and stir in the cheese. Cook for 15 minutes more and ladle into bowls. Serve as it is or drizzle with oil.

14. Exotic Chicken Dish

Ingredients
- 3 pounds chicken breast
- 3 cups red bell peppers, cut into smaller chunks
- 3 cups mango chunks
- 2 cups olive oil
- 1 cup white wine
- 6 tablespoons yogurt
- 6 tablespoons pineapple juice, homemade or unsweetened
- 1 tablespoon ginger, garlic and pumpkin spice, each
- Green lettuce leaves to garnish

Method
1. In a large skillet, brown the chicken on all sides for about 8 minutes.
2. Add the meat along with the remaining ingredients except for the mango and peppers to the slow cooker and cook for 6 hours on low heat.
3. Add the mangoes and peppers and stir to combine well. Cook for another 2 hours on low temperature. Check the meat for doneness.
4. Uncover the slow cooker and continue cooking for about 30 minutes, allowing the sauce to reduce. Add salt to taste and serve as it is.

15. Chili Verde

Ingredients
- 1 cup beans, cooked
- 1 jar salsa verde
- 1 pound boneless, skinless chicken breast
- 2 ribs celery, chopped
- 1 onion, chopped
- 2 cloves garlic, minced
- 1 green bell pepper, chopped
- 8 ounces Monterey Jack cheese
- 1/2 cup chopped cilantro
- 1 teaspoon oregano and ground cumin, each
- 12 corn tortillas, cut into 6 wedges

Method
1. Place the chicken and veggies into the slow cooker. Add the seasonings and top with salsa verde.
2. Turn the slow cooker on and cook for 6 to 8 hours on low temperature.
3. After 7 hours, add the beans and shred the chicken with a fork. Continue cooking for 1 hour on low temperature.
4. Meanwhile, preheat the oven to 400°F. Place the tortillas on a baking sheet, coat them with cooking spray and bake for 2 to 3 minutes, until crips.
5. Serve the chili with the tortillas and cilantro.

16. Mac & Cheese

Ingredients
- 2 cups gluten-free pasta
- 4 ounces goat cheese
- 1 pound ground turkey
- 2 cups grated cheddar cheese
- 1 can kidney beans
- 1 can diced tomatoes, drained
- 1 onion, chopped
- 1 tablespoon olive oil
- 1 clove garlic, minced
- 2 teaspoons chili powder
- Pinch salt and cumin

Method
1. In a skillet, heat the oil and saute the onion and garlic. Add the turkey and cook for 5 minutes on each side, or until no longer pink.
2. Coat the slow cooker with cooking spray and add the turkey mixture. Stir in the beans, tomatoes, cumin, salt and chili powder. Cook on low temperature for 4 hours. 3. Meanwhile, in a pot, bring water to a boil and add the pasta. Boil for 10 minutes, then transfer the pasta to the slow cooker. Cook for 1 hour more, on low temperature.
3. Stir in the cheeses and let stand for a couple of minutes, to cool down. Serve as it is.

17. Hungarian Soup

Ingredients

- 2 pounds russet potatoes, cut into smaller cubes
- 1 cup skim milk
- 4 cups veggie broth, unsalted
- 1 onion, finely chopped
- 2 tablespoons chopped fresh dill
- 1/2 cup corn
- 1 tablespoon olive oil
- 1 teaspoon celery seeds
- 1 tablespoon paprika
- 1/2 teaspoon salt
- 1/4 teaspoon ground nutmeg
- Pepper to taste

Method

1. Place the potatoes, veggie broth, celery seeds and paprika into the slow cooker. Stir to combine well.
2. In a skillet, heat the oil and saute the onion until translucent, then add it to the slow cooker. Turn the slow cooker on, cooking for 4 to 6 hours on low temperature.
3. Check if the potatoes are tender and break them with a fork. Add the dill, salt, pepper and nutmeg and stir in the milk. Cook for 30 minutes more, on low temperature.

18. Smoky Soup

Ingredients
- 1 pound black beans
- 2 carrots
- 1 red bell pepper, chopped
- 1 dried chipotle chile pepper
- 3 ribs celery, chopped
- 1 onion, chopped
- 1 cup chopped cilantro
- 3 cloves garlic, minced
- 4 cups queso cheese, shredded
- 5 cups water
- 1 teaspoon dried oregano
- 1 teaspoon ground cumin
- Sour cream, optionally

Method
1. Add the beans into a bowl, cover with water and let soak overnight. Drain and rinse.
2. Place the beans in the slow cooker, together with the celery, carrots, pepper, onion, garlic, chipotle, oregano, cumin and water. Turn the slow cooker on and cook on low temperature for 6 to 7 hours.
3. Check if the beans are tender, discard the chipotle pepper and transfer the soup to a food processor. Add the cheese and puree to obtain a smooth and thick soup, working in batches.

F.L.Clover

4. Once done, return the soup to the slow cooker and cook for 1 hour more. Stir in the sour cream and cilantro and serve as it is.

19. French Onion Soup

Ingredients
- 3 onions, thinly sliced
- 4 cups veggie broth
- 1 cup Parmesan cheese
- 2 tablespoons rice flour
- 2 tablespoons olive oil
- 2 tablespoons butter
- 1 teaspoon sugar
- 1 teaspoon salt
- 1/2 cup dry white wine, optionally
- 8 slices rice bread, gluten-free

Method
1. In a large skillet, heat the oil and butter over medium heat and add the onions. Saute for 5 minutes, add the sugar and salt and cook for 10 more minutes. Add the flour and cook for 5 minutes, stirring.
2. Move the mixture into the slow cooker, add wine and broth and cook on low temperature, for 6 to 8 hours.
3. Toast the bread, sprinkle with cheese and broil until golden. Serve the soup topped with the cheese toast.

20. Salmon Pasta Casserole

Ingredients
- 6 ounces corn pasta, gluten free
- 1 can salmon, drained
- 1 can artichoke hearts, drained, chopped
- 2 scallions, chopped
- 2 tomatoes, cut into smaller pieces
- 1 cup Parmesan cheese, grated
- 1/4 cup canola oil
- 1 tablespoon lemon juice
- Water

Method
1. Add the pasta, artichoke, scallions and canola oil in the slow cooker and cover with water. Cook on low temperature for 2 hours.
2. Stir in the salmon, lemon juice and cheese and continue cooking for another hour, on low temperature.
3. Transfer to serving plates, stir in the tomatoes and mix to incorporate well. Serve warm.

Chapter Three: Dinner Recipes

1. Turkey Chili

Ingredients
- 1 pound turkey meat
- 1 can kidney beans, cooked
- 1 can pinto beans, cooked
- 1 can diced tomatoes
- 1 onion, diced
- 2 bell peppers, diced
- 2 stalks celery, diced
- 2 teaspoons ground cumin
- 1 tablespoon chili powder
- 1/2 cup cheddar cheese, grated
- Salt to taste
- Olive oil

Method
1. In a skillet, heat some olive oil and lightly brown the turkey for 5 minutes on each side. Break into smaller parts with a fork and set aside.
2. Coat the slow cooker with cooking spray. Add the onion, beans, tomatoes, pepper, celery and herbs to the slow cooker and layer the meat on top of them. Turn the slow cooker on and cook on low for 8 to 10 hours.
3. Transfer to plates and serve topped with cheese.

2. Orange Chicken

Ingredients
- 4 pounds chicken breast, chopped
- 1/2 cup chicken broth
- 1 pound asparagus, cut into small pieces
- 1/2 cup plain yogurt
- 1 bell pepper, chopped
- 2 cloves garlic, minced
- 1 onion, cut into wedges
- 1/4 cup water
- 3 tablespoons orange juice
- 1 teaspoon dried thyme
- 1/2 cup almonds

Method
1. Add the onion, pepper and garlic into the slow cooker and pour the broth and orange juice on top. Add the thyme and place the chicken over these ingredients, then mix to coat the meat well on all sides.
2. Cook for 3 to 4 hours on low temperature, then add the asparagus and water and cook for 1 hour more, or until the veggie is done.
3. Transfer to plates and serve with yogurt and almonds on top.

3. Pumpkin Parsnip Soup

Ingredients
- 1 large pumpkin, peeled, diced
- 1 onion, sliced
- 2 parsnips, diced
- 1 clove garlic, minced
- 1 tablespoon ginger, minced
- 2 tablespoons coconut oil
- 1/2 teaspoon cumin, cilantro and salt, each
- 2 cups veggie stock
- Chives and ham, optionally

Method
1. Add the pumpkin and parsnip into the slow cooker.
2. In a large saucepan, heat the oil and simmer the onion, garlic and spices for 10 minutes, stirring occasionally. Add the stock and bring to a boil.
3. Transfer the mixture into the slow cooker, add more water if needed and salt to taste and cook for 6 to 8 hours on low. Serve as it is or garnish with chives and ham.

4. Beef Carnitas

Ingredients
- 2 pounds beef meat, cut into cubes
- 1 cup beef stock or water
- 2 tablespoons chopped chipotle chili peppers
- 3/4 cup salsa, mild
- Pinch salt and pepper
- Gluten-free tortilla, optionally

Method
1. Add all the ingredients into the slow cooker, cover and cook on low for 6 to 8 hours. Serve as it is or layer it onto a gluten free tortilla.

5. Potato Ham Chowder

Ingredients
- 4 cups potatoes, diced
- 3 cups chicken broth
- 1 cup cubed ham steak
- 2 cups heavy cream
- 1 cup chopped onion
- 2 cloves garlic, chopped
- 1 teaspoon salt
- Pinch black pepper

Method
1. Place all the ingredients into the slow cooker, except for the heavy cream, and turn to low, cooking for 6 to 7 hours.
2. Add the cream, then cook for another hour on low temperature. Top with cheese and green onion or serve as it is.

6. Creamy Kale Chicken

Ingredients
- 4 chicken breasts, cut into chunks
- 2 cans tomatoes in sauce
- 1 can black beans
- 1 onion, cut into strips
- 4 cups kale, chopped
- 80 ounces cream cheese
- 1 teaspoon garlic powder
- 1 teaspoon salt
- 1/2 teaspoon pepper
- 1 teaspoon seasoning of your taste

Method
1. Add the chicken, onion, tomatoes, kale, beans and spices into the slow cooker, add water as needed to cover the ingredients and cook for 4 hours on low temperature, stirring occasionally. Check every hour to see whether the kale is well covered with water and add more water if needed.
2. Add the cream cheese and cook for 30 minutes more. Season and serve warm.

7. Mexican Cauliflower Soup

Ingredients
- One head cauliflower, stems removed, cut into small chunks
- 2 bell peppers, diced
- 1 onion, diced
- 1 cup tomato sauce
- 1/2 cup chicken stock
- 1 tablespoon tomato paste
- 2 jalapeno peppers, diced
- 1 clove garlic, minced
- 2 teaspoons oregano and ground cumin, each
- Salt and pepper to taste

Method
1. Add the chicken stock, tomato sauce and tomato paste to the slow cooker, add the spices and stir to mix well. Add the peppers and onion, then the cauliflower and stir everything until the cauliflower is well coated. Add more water if needed, to cover all ingredients.
2. Turn the slow cooker on to low heat and cook for 5 to 6 hours. Using a spatula, mash all the ingredients to obtain smaller pieces or transfer the soup to a food processor and mix to obtain s puree. Serve as it is or fridge overnight, it will have a stronger flavor.

8. Mashed Cauliflower

Ingredients
- 1 large head of cauliflower
- 1 package fresh dill
- 6 cloves of garlic
- Salt and pepper to taste
- Splash or coconut milk

Method
1. Cut the cauliflower into florets and add it to the slow cooker, add the garlic, dill and coconut milk, season with salt and pepper and add enough water to cover the ingredients.
2. Turn the slow cooker on and cook for 6 to 8 hours on low temperature, checking from time to time and adding more water if needed. Serve as it is or refrigerate and serve cool with dill and cheese on top.

9. Citrus Turkey

Ingredients
- 1 pound turkey or chicken breast
- 3 cloves garlic, minced
- 1 cup chicken broth
- 1 piece ginger (2 inches), grated
- 1 onion, chopped
- 2 teaspoons coconut oil
- 1 can diced tomatoes
- 1/4 cup lemon juice
- Salt and pepper to taste
- Sliced oranges, optionally

Method
1. Heat 1 teaspoon coconut oil into a pan over medium heat and place the turkey, seasoning with salt and pepper. Brown on all sides and transfer to a plate.
2. In the same pan, add the onion and brown it, then set aside.
3. Add the remaining coconut oil into the slow cooker, stir in the ginger, garlic, lemon juice, onion, chicken broth and turkey and season to taste. Cook for 1 hour on medium temperature, stirring occasionally.
4. Add the tomatoes and cook for 3-4 hours on low temperature. Serve as it is or with sliced oranges. Goes well with brown rice.

10. Buttery Chicken

Ingredients
- 4 chicken thighs, cut into small pieces
- 1 cup tomato sauce
- 1 cup diced tomatoes
- 1 tin coconut milk
- 1/2 cup butter
- 1 onion, diced
- 1 cup plain yogurt
- 3 cloves garlic, minced
- 2 tablespoons coconut oil
- Salt and pepper to taste

Method
1. In a pan, melt the butter and oil over medium heat. Stir in the chicken, onion and garlic and cook until the onion is soften, for about 10 minutes. Add the tomato paste and cook for 10 minutes.
2. Transfer the mixture into the slow cooker, add the remaining ingredients, season to taste and let cook for 6 to 8 hours, on low temperature. If needed, add water from time to time, to obtain the desired consistency for the sauce covering the chicken.

11. Pumpkin Chili

Ingredients
- 1 pound ground beef
- 1 cup chicken stock
- 2 cans diced green chiles
- 2 potatoes, cut into small cubes
- 2 cloves garlic, minced
- 1 onion, diced
- 2 bell peppers, diced
- 1 can diced tomatoes
- 1 can pumpkin
- 1 teaspoon cinnamon and chili powder, each
- Salt and pepper to taste

Method
1. Add all the ingredients into the slow cooker and cook on low temperature, for 6 to 8 hours or until the meat is cooked through. Transfer to plates and serve as it is, or top with cheddar cheese.

12. Jack Chicken

Ingredients
- 1 pound chicken breast, cut into smaller parts
- 1 can black beans, rinsed and drained
- 1 can white salsa
- 1 cup monterey jack cheese
- 1/4 cup chopped cilantro
- 1/2 teaspoon ground cumin and dried oregano, each

Method
1. Add all the ingredients except for the chicken into the slow cooker and mix to incorporate well. Place the meat on top, season to taste and add water for a thinner consistency.
2. Turn the slow cooker on and cook for 6 to 8 hours on low temperature. Transfer the meat to plates and top with sauce and extra cheese.

13. Spicy Shrimp with Rice

Ingredients
- 1 pound frozen shrimp
- 2 cans tomato sauce, unsalted
- 1 can diced tomatoes
- 1 cup rice of your preference, uncooked
- 1 onion, diced
- 2 cups water
- 1 packet mixed veggies stir fry
- 1 teaspoon paprika, black pepper, garlic and salt each

Method
1. Add the veggies, tomato sauce, rice, onion, diced tomatoes and water into the slow cooker. Season to taste and cook for one hour on low temperature.
2. Meanwhile, let the frozen shrimp in water to defrost. Transfer the shrimp to the slow cooker after the first hour and cook for 3-4 hours more, on low temperature. Serve as it is.

14. Four Bean Stew

Ingredients
- 1 can black bean soup
- 1 can garbanzo beans
- 1 can white beans
- 1 can corn
- 1 can kidney beans
- 2 stalks celery, chopped
- 1 onion, chopped
- 1 can chopped tomatoes
- 1 bell pepper, chopped
- 2 cloves garlic, chopped
- 1 tablespoon dried oregano, parsley and basil, each
- Salt and pepper to taste

Method
1. In a slow cooker, combine the beans, soup, corn, tomatoes, onion and celery. Stir to incorporate well and add the garlic, bell pepper and seasonings. Add salt and pepper to taste.
2. Add water to cover the ingredients well and turn the slow cooker on, cooking for 6 to 8 hours on low temperature. Serve topped with sour cream or as it is.

15. Split Pea Sausage Stew

Ingredients
- 1 pound split peas, dried
- 2 potatoes, chopped
- 1 cup chopped celery
- 1 pound sausage of your choice
- 1 cup chopped carrot
- 2 bay leaves
- 1/2 teaspoon garlic powder and oregano, each
- 10 cups water
- 5 cubes chicken bouillon or 3 tablespoons tomato paste

Method
1. Add all the ingredients into the slow cooker and add water on top to cover them well. Turn the slow cooker on to low temperature and cook for 6 to 8 hours.
2. Remove the bay leaves and transfer to plates. Serve with sour cream on top.

16. Beef Stroganoff

Ingredients
- 1 pound beef, cubed
- 4 ounces cream cheese
- 1 tablespoon Worcestershire sauce
- 1 onion, chopped
- 1 can mushroom soup, unsalted, unsweetened
- 1/4 cup water

Method
1. Add the meat, soup, onion, Worcestershire sauce and water in the slow cooker. Turn the temperature to low and cook for 7 to 8 hours, stirring occasionally.
2. After 6 hours, add half of the cheese cream and cook for the remaining time. Transfer to plates, top with cheese and serve warm, with rice alongside.

17. Turkey Cranberry Stew

Ingredients
- 3 pounds turkey drumsticks, skin removed
- 1 cup chicken stock
- 1/2 cup dried cranberries
- 1 pound sweet potatoes, cut into small chunks
- 1 onion, diced
- 1 tablespoon honey
- 1 tablespoon cider vinegar
- 2 tablespoons gluten-free flour
- 1 teaspoon salt
- Pinch black pepper

Method
1. Add the turkey, onion and stock to the slow cooker. Add the vinegar and all the seasonings, then cook on low temperature for 5 hours.
2. Stir in the cranberries and potatoes. Cook for 1 hour more and check if the potatoes are tender. Stir in the flour, cooking for 30 minutes more, uncovered, and stirring frequently.
3. Toss the meat and potatoes, transfer to plates and serve warm, with sourdough gluten-free bread.

18. Shrimp Arrabiata

Ingredients
- 1 pound shrimp, peeled, deveined
- 1 can tomatoes in puree
- 6 ounces gluten-free pasta, cooked
- 3 cloves garlic, minced
- 1 bell pepper, chopped
- 1 onion, chopped
- 1 teaspoon oregano and basil, each

Method
1. In a bowl, mix the tomatoes with sauce and seasonings, to obtain a thick consistency. Add the garlic, bell pepper and seasonings into the slow cooker and pour the mixture on top.
2. Add water to cover the ingredients and cook on low temperature for 4 to 6 hours. Stir in the shrimp and cook for 1 more hour on low temperature.
3. Divide along plates and serve with cooked gluten-free pasta.

19. Pork Chops

Ingredients
- 6 boneless pork chops
- 2 cloves garlic, crushed
- 1/4 cup tomato sauce, unsalted
- 1/4 cup brown sugar
- 1/2 cup sour cream
- 1 teaspoon ground ginger
- Salt and pepper to taste

Method
1. Place the pork chops into the slow cooker.
2. In a bowl, combine the remaining ingredients and mix to incorporate well, then pour this mixture over the meat. Cook on low temperature for 6 to 8 hours, adding water if needed and checking the meat for doneness after 3-4 hours. Adjust the water amount as needed during the cooking time.
3. Transfer to plates, let cool for 5-10 minutes and serve over fried rice.

20. Onion and Corn

Ingredients
- 4 cup corn, gluten-free
- 1/2 cup half-and-half
- 1/4 cup butter, unsalted, melted
- 4 slices bacon
- 1 red bell pepper
- 1 onion
- 1 container onion cream cheese
- 1 teaspoon brown sugar
- 1/2 teaspoon salt
- Pinch pepper

Method
1. Melt the butter in a pan, add the onion and lightly brown it. Add the half-and-half, mix and simmer for 3-4 minutes.
2. Put the bacon, bell pepper, corn, cream cheese, sugar and onion mixture in the slow cooker. Add water to cover the 2/3 of the ingredients and season to taste. Turn to low temperature and cook for 4 to 6 hours.
3. Transfer to plates and serve as it is or with plain green veggies.

*Corn is gluten free, but some products are cross-contaminated, so make sure to check the label for no gluten.

Chapter Four: Desserts & Beverages

1. Baked Apples

Ingredients
- 6 green apples, large
- 1/4 cup raisins
- 6 tablespoons coconut oil or butter
- 1/4 cup honey
- 1 teaspoon cinnamon

Method
1. Core the apples, making room for the filling.
2. In a small bowl, mix the cinnamon, raisins, honey and coconut oil. Fill the apples with this mixture and place them in the slow cooker, adding 1/2 inch of water.
3. Turn the slow cooker on and let it cook for 8 hours on low temperature. Serve the baked apples as they are or with yogurt, cream or ice-cream on top.

2. Date Pudding

Ingredients
- 1/4 cup chopped dates
- 1 cup oats
- 3 cups water
- 1/2 teaspoon coconut butter
- 1 tablespoon coconut powder
- 1/2 teaspoon ground cinnamon
- Cooking spray or coconut oil

Method
1. Coat the slow cooker with cooking spray or coconut oil and add the oats, dates, butter, cinnamon, coconut powder and water.
2. Turn the slow cooker on and let cook for 4 to 6 hours on low temperature. When ready, top with extra coconut powder or serve as it is.

*Make sure to check the oats for a gluten-free label, some products might be cross-contaminated.

3. Brownie Squares

Ingredients
- 2/3 cup almond flour
- 1/2 cup unsweetened cacao powder
- 1 beetroot, grated
- 1/3 cup coconut butter
- 2/3 cup almond milk
- 2/3 cup sugar
- 1 teaspoon baking powder
- 1 egg, lightly beaten
- 1 cup mini chocolate chips, semisweet
- 1 teaspoon vanilla extract
- 1/4 teaspoon salt

Method
1. Coat the slow cooker with cooking spray and add the flour, cacao, beetroot, sugar, baking powder and salt. Stir to incorporate well, then add the liquid ingredients and mix to obtain a smooth composition.
2. Add the chocolate chips and mix again, spreading the mixture evenly in the slow cooker. When ready, turn the temperature to low and let cook for 3 to 4 hours or until the composition is set. You can test with a wooden pick in the middle, and it should come out clean.
3. Turn off the slow cooker and let the brownie cool for 15 minutes, uncovered. Slice and serve as it is.

4. Strawberry Rhubarb Crisps

Ingredients
- 4 cups chopped rhubarb
- 4 cups chopped strawberries
- 1 cup oats, gluten-free
- 3/4 cup almond flour
- 1/4 cup coconut butter
- 1/2 cup brown sugar
- 2 tablespoons tapioca
- 1 teaspoon cinnamon
- 1/2 teaspoon ginger
- Pinch salt

Method
1. Coat the slow cooker with cooking spray and add the rhubarb, strawberries, tapioca, sugar, ginger and cinnamon. Toss to incorporate well and cook on medium temperature for 30 minutes.
2. Meanwhile, in a bowl, add the oats, flour, salt and butter and form crumbs. Add these into the slow cooker, switch to low temperature and cook for 3 to 4 hours or until the rhubarb is tender.
3. Transfer to plates and let cool for a couple of minutes, then serve as it is or with whipped cream.

5. Applesauce

Ingredients
- 2 pounds apples, chopped
- 2 cups water
- 1 tablespoon cinnamon
- 1 teaspoon apple cider vinegar
- 1/4 teaspoon nutmeg

Method
1. Add the apples, cinnamon, apple cider vinegar and nutmeg into the slow cooker and mix to incorporate well. Add the water and turn the slow cooker to low temperature.
2. Cook for 1 hour, then check to see if there's enough water inside. Add more if needed, and cook for another 3-4 hours on low temperature. Check the consistency from time to time and adjust the amount of water as needed. For extra flavor, add more cinnamon.

6. Coconut Cherry Bars

Ingredients
- 1 cup coconut butter
- 2 eggs
- 1/3 cup brown sugar
- 1 cup almond flour
- 1/2 cup cherries
- 1/2 cup almonds, sliced
- 1/2 teaspoon almond extract
- 1/2 cup shredded coconut
- 1 package chocolate chips
- Pinch salt

Method
1. Coat the slow cooker with cooking spray.
2. In a saucepan, melt the butter over medium heat and add 1 cup of chocolate chips, but don't stir. Set aside and allow to melt.
3. Meanwhile, in another bowl, add the eggs and beat until foamy. Incorporate the sugar and flour gradually, and mix to obtain a smooth composition. Add the salt and almond extract and mix again until well blended.
4. Pour half of this composition into the slow cooker and turn it on, cooking for 30 minutes on medium temperature. Add the coconut and the remaining chocolate chips and cook again for 30 minutes, on low temperature.
5. Pour the remaining batter, almond and cherries and cook for 3 to 4 hours, on low temperature. Sprinkle with coconut and let cool for 1 hour, then serve as it is.

Gluten Free Slow Cooker Cookbook

7. PB Chocolate Cake

Ingredients
- 1 1/2 cup almond flour
- 1/2 cup coconut flakes
- 1 cup peanut butter, creamy
- 1/2 cup cocoa, unsweetened
- 3/4 cup sour cream
- 3/4 cup brown sugar
- 1 teaspoon baking soda
- 1 teaspoon baking powder
- 1 teaspoon almond extract
- 3 tablespoons coconut butter, melted
- 2 cups boiling water
- 2 tablespoons peanut butter, melted
- 2 tablespoons almonds, chopped

Method
1. Coat the slow cooker with cooking spray.
2. In a bowl, whisk the flour, sugar, baking soda and baking powder. Add the peanut butter and sour cream and mix to incorporate well. Add the melted butter and almond extract, mixing again to form a thick batter. Transfer the batter into the slow cooker.

F.L.Clover

3. In a separate bowl, whisk the cocoa powder with the coconut flakes and 2 cups of boiling water and combine until you obtain a smooth mixture, then pour this mixture over the batter in the slow cooker.
4. Turn the temperature to low and cook for 2 to 3 hours. Check to see if the sides of the cake are firm and cook for another hour if needed, checking with a wooden stick the middle and sides.
5. When ready, drizzle with melted peanut butter and almonds, allow to cool for 15-20 minutes and serve.

8. Dulce de Leche

Ingredients
- 2 cans sweetened condensed milk

Method
1. Do not open the milk cans but remove the labels. Once done, place the cans into the slow cooker and add water to cover 3/4 up the cans.
2. Turn the temperature on high and cook for 6 hours, then remove from the slow cooker and let cool at room temperature.
3. Open the cans, scrape out the milk and serve as it is or refrigerate for one hour and serve cool. Should have caramel's consistency and flavor.

9. Apricot Cherry Compote

Ingredients
- 4 pears, cut into small cubes
- 1 cup cherries
- 1 cup apricots
- 1/2 cup green grapes
- 1/2 cup brown sugar
- 2 1/4 cups hot water
- 1/2 teaspoon vanilla extract
- 1 teaspoon orange zest
- Pinch salt

Method
1. Add the water, sugar and salt into the slow cooker and mix to incorporate well, until the sugar is dissolved. Add the fruits and vanilla, turn the temperature to low and cook for 5 hours.
2. Check to see if the fruits are tender Cook for 1 hour more if needed, on low temperature.

10. Apple Mulled Cider

Ingredients
- 6 cups apple juice
- 4 cinnamon sticks
- 3 cups cranberry juice
- 1/2 cup cranberries
- 1 apple, cut into small cubes
- 1 orange, sliced
- 1/4 cup honey
- 1 tablespoon ginger
- 1/2 teaspoon cloves
- 1/4 teaspoon nutmeg

Method
1. Pour all the juices into the slow cooker and add the spices and cranberries. Add the cinnamon sticks, orange and apple, then turn the slow cooker on to low temperature.
2. Let it cook for 4 to 6 hours and taste. Keep in mind that cooking for longer means a stronger flavor, so if you're not into spicy cider, let it cook only for 4 hours.
3. Pour into cups and serve with honey.

F.L.Clover

Conclusions

Gluten-free recipes are not just tasty, but healthy as well. Switching to a GF diet can help in improving your overall health state, as foods containing gluten tend to interfere with the absorption of nutrients and cause digestion issues. Once removing this ingredient from your meals, you might notice quick improvements in your appearance and body composition, as a better nourished body is a healthier and better looking one!

Gluten is one of the anti-nutrients found in lots of grains and grain products, and the term "anti-nutrient" is self-explanatory: this tiny protein, although tolerated by some people, can irritate the membrane lining the intestinal tract, causing bloating, stomach cramps and pain, digestive discomfort and even more severe symptoms. Also, it can affect the aspect of your skin, making it more prone to acne outbreaks.

These signs are the result of gluten intolerance, condition which is very common but often neglected. After adopting a gluten-free diet, not only you'll experience less frequent digestive issues, but your skin's health will also improve, and blood will start carrying higher amounts of nutrients to cells, so your energy levels will be restored. This will lead, consequently, to less frequent hunger pangs, a healthier appetite and a better control of your sugar cravings. Not to mention it will also be easier to lose the extra weight, as a better absorption of nutrients prevents overeating.

Although you can find lots of gluten-free desserts, pastries, cereals and breads on the market, we strongly advise you to stick with homemade dishes, as this way you can control all the ingredients and keep away the unnecessary chemicals that are often added in commercial products.

We hope this book will encourage and motivate you to switch to a gluten-free diet and experience the numerous health benefits of this new lifestyle!

Gluten Free Slow Cooker Cookbook

Photo credits

Logo by Alexkava,
http://www.shutterstock.com/pic.mhtml?id=83515909

Peach oatmeal, Yulia Davidovich,
http://www.dreamstime.com/stock-photography-oatmeal-
caramelized-peaches-bowl-jug-yogurt-breakfast-close-up-horizontal-
image33839062

Congee, Kheng Guan Toh, http://www.dreamstime.com/royaly-free-
stock-photograpy-chinese-proddige-image4006407

Cherry oatmeal, Alein,
http://www.123rf.com/photo_21454087_oatmeal-porridge-with-
cherries.html

Quinoa casserole, Eunice,
https://www.flickr.com/photos/ejchang/5116124980/

Pumpkin cinnamon oatmeal, Vanessa P.,
https://www.flickr.com/photos/thevelvetbird/51251227860/

Blueberry clafoutis, Jim Champion,
https://www.flickr.com/photos/treehouse1977/7685901142

Pear butter, Jennifer Feuchter,
https://www.flickr.com/photos/jennerosity/10719053185/

Chocolate risotto, Maggie,
http://www.flickr.com/photos/maggiejane/3199890233/

Maple walnut oatmeal, Carly Lesser & Art Drauglis,
https://www.flickr.com/photos/wiredwitch/4448961596/

Spinach and ham casserole, MShev,
http://www.shutterstock.com/pic.mhtml?id=150411800&src=id

F.L.Clover

Beef and cabbage, Arfo,
http://www.123rf.com/photo_25270894_traditional-polish-sauerkraut-bigos-with-mushrooms-and-cranberries.html

Cheesy chicken, Anna Kvach,
http://www.123rf.com/photo_19912053_bowl-of-chicken-and-roasted-mushrooms.html

Lentil soup, Robert Judge,
https://www.flickr.com/photos/bobjudge/2239087919/

Salsa pork tenderloin, Joselu Blanco,
https://www.flickr.com/photos/silverman68/7190823788/

Chicken dumpling soup, Jordanmit09,
https://www.flickr.com/photos/jordansorensen/3753677421/

Jambalaya, Jerry Pank,
https://www.flickr.com/photos/cookipedia/6781248637/

Sweet potatoes, Maria Komar, http://www.shutterstock.com/pic-80726200/stock-photo-roasted-potatoes-with-parsley-in-bowl.html

Pork chille, Andrew Lynch,
https://www.flickr.com/photos/newandrew/6158092194/

Split pea soup, Qfamily,
https://www.flickr.com/photos/dasqfamily/2213950065/

Turkey meatloaf, Razmarinka,
http://www.shutterstock.com/pic.mhtml?id=122320564&src=id

Stuffed peppers, William Andrus,
https://www.flickr.com/photos/wandrus/5697759851/

Slow cooker roast, Moramo Paraguna,
https://www.flickr.com/photos/94278227@N03/10877861295/

Bean soup, Sarah,
https://www.flickr.com/photos/dichohecho/3101362174/

Exotic chicken dish, Jeffreyww,
https://www.flickr.com/photos/hamburger_helper/favorites/with/488
9339470

Chili verde, Lesley Show,
https://www.flickr.com/photos/thelesleyshow/6697255305/

Mac&cheese, Gwen,
https://www.flickr.com/photos/theaudiochick/4984129439/

Hungarian soup, TopBudapestOrg,
https://www.flickr.com/photos/topbudapest/9368219362

Smoky soup, Warren Layton,
https://www.flickr.com/photos/34917178@N08/4590222729/

French onion soup, Stu_Spivack,
https://www.flickr.com/photos/stuart_spivack/73354413/

Salmon pasta casserole, Rool Paap,
https://www.flickr.com/photos/roolrool/4194836776

Turkey chili, Mary,
https://www.flickr.com/photos/maryamandathompson/5139284524/

Orange chicken, Bev Sykes,
https://www.flickr.com/photos/basykes/162230477

Pumpkin parsnip soup, Q Family,
https://www.flickr.com/photos/dasqfamily/2218090957/

Beef carnitas, Toshihiro Gamo,
https://www.flickr.com/photos/dakiny/4462342070

Potato ham chowder, Jay del Corro,
https://www.flickr.com/photos/ramenfuel/6860436957/

Creamy kale chicken, Dollen,
https://www.flickr.com/photos/dollen/11896133214

F.L.Clover

Mexican cauliflower soup, Devika,
https://www.flickr.com/photos/devika_smile/10020764796/

Mashed cauliflower, David Reber,
https://www.flickr.com/photos/davidreber/9380484270/

Citrus turkey, Rexipe Rexipe,
https://www.flickr.com/photos/rexipe/1124524113/

Buttery chicken, Stu_spivack,
https://www.flickr.com/photos/35034346243@N01/2284519526

Pumpkin chili, Alpha,
https://www.flickr.com/photos/avlxyz/4591227453/

Jack chicken, Steve Dunham,
https://www.flickr.com/photos/dunham/5121843581/

Spicy shrimp with rice, Jeffreyw,
https://www.flickr.com/photos/jeffreyww/8318182455/

Four bean stew, Erik Burton,
https://www.flickr.com/photos/13470115@N08/6734016371

Split pea sausage stew, Fiona Henderson,
https://www.flickr.com/photos/fifikins/2348515559/

Beef stroganoff, Naotake Murayama,
https://www.flickr.com/photos/naotakem/4015894224

Turkey cranberry stew, Shannon Clark,
https://www.flickr.com/photos/shannonclark/304830582/

Shrimp arrabiata, Dan Zen,
https://www.flickr.com/photos/danzen/294062949/

Pork chops, Alpha,
https://www.flickr.com/photos/avlxyz/4730337310/

Gluten Free Slow Cooker Cookbook

Onion and corn, Steven Depolo,
https://www.flickr.com/photos/stevendepolo/8367415849

Baked apples, Eunice,
https://www.flickr.com/photos/ejchang/365298820/

Date pudding, Laurent,
https://www.flickr.com/photos/loloieg/3733667317/

Brownie squares, Sarah,
https://www.flickr.com/photos/8978957@N07/3062117056/

Strawberry rhubarb crisps, Jessica Merz,
https://www.flickr.com/photos/jessicafm/158738247

Applesauce, Stacy,
https://www.flickr.com/photos/notahipster/4319957825/

Coconut cherry bars, Stephanie Frey,
http://www.dreamstime.com/stock-images-coconut-chocolate-chip-bars-image25887694

PB chocolate cake, Thebittenword,
https://www.flickr.com/photos/galant/3295312660

Dulce de leche, Kai Hendry,
https://www.flickr.com/photos/hendry/362655239

Apricot cherry compote, Luis Vidal,
https://www.flickr.com/photos/luisvidallois/9273098099/

Apple mulled cider, Msheldrake,
http://www.123rf.com/photo_5737755_hot-mulled-apple-cider-with-cinnamon-stick.html

F.L.Clover

Other books from F.L. Clover

If you enjoyed reading this book and preparing the tasty recipes here, please visit your favorite ebook retailer to discover other books by F.L. Clover:

Gluten Free 101 Recipes

Easy, healthy and delicious gluten-free cookbook for all occasions

By F.L.Clover

http://www.amazon.com/Gluten-Free-101-Delicious-Gluten-Free-ebook/dp/B00JG31O70

Gluten Free Slow Cooker Cookbook

Review Asking

Thank you again for downloading our book "Gluten-Free Slower Cooker Cookbook"! We hope this book was able to help you in preparing perfectly delicious and appealing gluten-free slow cooker recipes.

The next step is to take action. Now's the time to try out these recipes for yourself & start making your own variations to discover the perfect gluten-free meals which suit your needs!

Finally, if you enjoyed this book, please take the time to share your thoughts & post a review or your comments. It'd be significantly appreciated!

Thank you and good luck!

Printed in Great Britain
by Amazon